M000032694

THE LITTLE BOOK OF
BBQ

Published by OH!
20 Mortimer Street
London W1T 3JW

Disclaimer:

ISBN 978-1-80069-009-7

Compiled by: Malcolm Croft
Editorial: Lisa Dyer
Project manager: Russell Porter
Design: Tony Seddon
Production: Freencky Portas

A CIP catalogue record for this book is available from the British Library

Printed in Dubai

10 9 8 7 6 5 4 3 2 1

Illustrations: Freepik.com

THE LITTLE BOOK OF
BBQ

PERFECTLY GRILLED
WIT & WISDOM

CONTENTS

INTRODUCTION

The scratch, spark, and sniff of a match. The snap, crackle, and pop of burning wood. The hypnotic red-white glow of charcoal. The fragrant heat of woody smoke and ash. The mesmerizing dance of flames licking the air. The sizzle of meat as it first touches the grill. The smell of seasoning, herbs, and caramelizing meat. The lip-smacking smiles of giddy friends and family. That first sip of a cold beer on a hot day. That feeling of sweating profusely because you've eaten way, way, way, way too much.

Yep, we're talking about barbecue. What else is there? Nothing can fan our lusty flames of gastronomic nirvana as much as a bit of B, B, and Q.

This *Little Book of BBQ* is stuffed with a mouth-watering bonanza of barbecue brilliance, a tiny tome guaranteed to make more than a happy meal of its subject matter, a buffet of BBQ-based celebration that turns the heat all the way up to 11. And if you can't stand the heat, go grab the chef a beer.

Yes, this book contains all the bare-grill necessities you'll need to keep you cookin' on all cylinders, all in bitesize, easy-to-digest nuggets of knowledge. From pretenders to pitmasters, pyromaniacs to piggin' out, *The Little Book of BBQ* is the perfect spark to ignite your BBQ inspiration into a white hot frenzy—figuratively speaking, of course.

So, raise your tongs toward the sky, because it's time to tuck in to all that is tasty about the magic that happens when meat meets heat. Enjoy!

CHAPTER
ONE

Slow and Low

Have you ever heard the story about the hare and the tortoise?

The tortoise won the race because it took things slow and low.

And that's the essential of barbecue. It's about the juicy journey as much as the delicious destination. That said, if you want to cook hot and fast, go for it! The first rule of barbecue is ... break all the rules!

Ten Commandments of BBQ

1. Steak should always be cooked no more than medium rare.

2. Burgers must be eaten with hands, not cutlery.

3. Don't ask the chef about the salad.

4. There must be at least one vegetable on offer (as a token gesture).

5. Lighter fluid is *persona non grata*.

6. Chef eats first. And last.

7. Chef gets drinks brought directly to them.

8. No complaining about char ("adds to the taste").

9. One burger minimum.

10. No food gets left behind.

"

Barbecue may
not be the road to
world peace,
but it's a start.

"

Anthony Bourdain

Life is like a BBQ—don't stop until you've eaten *everything.*

66

Men like to
barbecue. Men will
cook if danger is
involved.

99

Rita Rudner

The American Dream

Barbecues are the gastronomic equivalent of the American Dream, aren't they?

In 2019, the total barbecue grill market in the United States was valued at a mouth-watering $2.54 billion. In that same year, approximately $1.36 billions worth of grills and barbecues were sold in the country.

The global barbecue grill market is forecast to be worth $6.5 billion by 2025.

Source: Statista

"

To barbecue is a
way of life rather
than a desirable
method of cooking.

"

Clement Freud

In the U.S., the most popular type of BBQ is the gas grill.

In 2019, they accounted for 61 percent of all grills sold in the country.

Source: Hearth, Patio, and Barbecue Association (HPBA)

This will come as no surprise to anyone, but the Fourth of July is the most popular American holiday for dusting off the BBQ. 73 percent of the nation celebrates with a BBQ.*

Source: Statista

* That's 255 million people. On one weekend.

66

Live fire cooking and barbecue have been so intimately linked with human evolution and history and politics. Everything we do, barbecue informs it in some way.

99

Steven Raichlen

Barbecoa

The first known instance of the word "barbecue" appearing in English print was in *A New Voyage Round the World* by buccaneer William Dampier, published in 1697. In his example, it referred to the structure as a place for sleeping: "And lay there all night, upon our Borbecu's, or frames of Sticks, raised about three foot from the ground."

Source: Live Science

The United States consumes more beef than any other country in the world. In one year, an average American consumer will eat approximately 200lbs (99kgs) of red meat.* That's around 4.5 servings of red meat a week.

In 2019, U.S. consumers spent more than $8 billion on red meat.

Source: BBC

For context, in the U.S., the average weight of a mature Angus beef cow is about 1,210 pounds.

"

Friends may
come and go,
but barbecues
accumulate.

"

Thomas Jones

"

Grilling, broiling, barbecuing—whatever you want to call it—is an art, not just a matter of building a pyre and throwing on a piece of meat as a sacrifice to the gods of the stomach.

"

James Beard

The average person devours approximately 3,200 calories at a BBQ. The average recommended daily allowance for calories is 2000 calories for women and 2,500 calories for men.

Source: Weight Watchers

Things People Say at a BBQ

1. Load it up.

2. I couldn't possibly have another one?
Oh, OK then . . .

3. Anyone for seconds?

4. I'm such a pig.

5. If you like your steak well done,
feel free to leave any time.

6. Compliments to the chef!

7. My bun is ready for your meat.

8. Diet starts tomorrow.

9. I hope you like them crispy.

10. The burn adds to the flavor.

Asado

The word for a barbecue
in Spanish.

"

The question is not
whether we will
barbecue, but how
we will barbecue.

"

Joan Z. Borysenko

BBQ Etiquette

BBQs are the height of sophistication, as you well know.

To avoid a social *faux pas* at your next BBQ, don't ask for ketchup.

Ask for a bottle of red. Keep it classy.

Burping

The process by which you swiftly and repeatedly open and close the lid of the BBQ a small amount, in order to generate a rush of oxygen inside the BBQ, which will reignite the hot gases.

The resulting fireball and/or reignition of flames is called a "flash-over."

Things You Overhear at a BBQ

"

I'm so hungry I could eat a horse.

"

The technical term for how you feel after you've eaten too much BBQ, and your body is dripping in protein-based perspiration, is known as the "meat sweats."

A symptom of meat sweats is "wet mouth." Congratulations, you will be soon in a beef-induced "Food Coma"!

Things You Overhear at a BBQ

"

BBQ makes
my eyes bigger than
my belly.

"

Broiling Vs. Grilling

Grilling:
The heat source is below.

Broiling:
The heat source is above.

"

My first outdoor cooking
memories are full of Dad
swearing at a barbecue
and eventually eating
charred sausages.

"

Jamie Oliver

The Chimney

The best way to light a charcoal BBQ is to create what is known as a "Chimney." You can do this using either a metal chimney device or, simply, stack your charcoal in the center of the BBQ in a pyramid shape, adding kindling, tinder, newspaper (or firelighters), among the stack. Once the coals are white, disperse evenly (or create two-zone cooking).

CHAPTER
TWO

Playing with Fire

There's something about being in the great outdoors, playing with fire, smelling of smoke, and feeling those intense heatwaves on our faces.

It all feels so . . . *natural*. Thanks to our ancestors, barbecuing is pure instinct to humans now; we're hardwired to use heat to cook and unable to live without it. It is part of our DNA. It's pure luck that it tastes so damn good, too.

Two-Zone Cooking
Direct Heat and Indirect Heat

Don't just lump your charcoal in the BBQ and hope you don't burn your meat to a crisp.

When your BBQ's charcoal is white hot, move all the charcoal to one side of the BBQ (for direct heat), leaving the other side of the BBQ clear (for indirect heat). This method allows more control of temperature and the ability to cook the interior and exterior of your meats separately and evenly.

Source: Barbecue Bible.com

"

There are no
ideas in the South,
just barbecue.

"

Pat Conroy

BBQ Slang

EVOO:
Extra Virgin Olive Oil.

"

Let's drown that bad boy
in EVOO.

"

The classic dry rub seasoning that consists solely of salt and black pepper is known, wonderfully, as the Dalmatian Rub.*

Your wife will call it the Clooney, after George Clooney's salt-and-pepper hair.

Beer Safe

The technical term for a BBQ recipe that's simple enough to prepare while drinking beer.

"

Barbecue is the
third rail of North
Carolina politics.

"

John Shelton Reed

66

There are two different things:
There's grilling, and there's
barbecue. Grilling is when people
say, 'We're going to turn up the
heat, make it really hot, and sear
a steak, sear a burger, cook a
chicken.' Barbecue is going
low and slow.

99

Guy Fieri

Globally, the amount
of meat produced
today is four times
more than it was 50
years ago.

Source: World Economic Forum

"

The price of barbecue is eternal vigilance.

"

Thomas Jefferson

"

A barbecue is just
the ultimate blokes'
pastime, isn't it?

"

Curtis Stone

Top Eight Meat-Eating Nations

1. United States 219 / 99

2. Australia 203 / 92

3. Argentina 198 / 89

4. Israel 195 / 88

5. Brazil 170 / 77

6. New Zealand 165 / 75

7. Chile 164 / 74

8. Canada 152 / 68

Source: World Economic Forum

*Pounds / Kilograms per capita, 2019.

Most Americans use their grill for an average of three years before replacing or upgrading.

Source: Seriously Smoked.com

"

If summer had one defining scent, it'd definitely be the smell of barbecue.

"

Katie Lee

2:1

The ratio of males
to females who
do all the "cooking"*
at BBQs.

Source: Seriously Smoked.com

Stand and watch.

62 percent of women will experimentwith more recipes and food with their BBQs, compared to only 50 percent of men.

Source: Seriously Smoked.com

3-2-1

When it comes to ribs,
remember the 3-2-1 rule.

Three hours in smoke.

Two hours wrapped
in foil.

One hour back in
the smoke.

Icon of BBQ:
Homer Simpson

Homer Simpson, the dysfunctional dad of
The Simpsons clan, is, without a doubt, America's best
example of BBQ hero. He loves them. These are his
favorite BBQ-based moments of brilliance.

Homer: Are you saying you're never going to
eat any animal again? What about bacon?

Lisa: No.

Homer: Ham?

Lisa: No.

Homer: Pork chops?

Lisa: Dad, those all come from the same animal.

Homer: Heh, heh, heh. Ooh, yeah, right, Lisa.
A wonderful, magical animal.

The Simpsons, 'Lisa the Vegetarian'

"Mmm . . . *barbecue*."

Homer, *The Simpsons*, 'When Flanders Failed'

Lisa: Come to Homer's BBBQ.
The extra B is for BYOBB.
Bart: Hey, Homer, what's that B for?
Homer: That's a typo.

***The Simpsons*, 'Lisa the Vegetarian'**

"But all normal people love meat. If I went
to a barbecue and there was no meat, I
would say 'Yo Goober! Where's the meat?!'
You don't win friends with salad."

Homer, *The Simpsons*, 'Lisa the Vegetarian'

In the U.S., approximately nine billion chickens are consumed each year.

Source: PETA

The word "barbecue" is used as a noun, verb, and adjective.

Barbecue—an event (noun)

Barbecue—a method of cooking (verb)

Barbecue—prepare meat for barbecuing (adjective)

The word first appeared in print in 1672, as a verb, in the writings of American John Lederer, which journaled his travels from Virginia, to the west of Carolina in 1669-70.

The word "flame" comes from the Latin *flamma*.*

FYI: In barbecuing, if you're "flame grilling" your meat, you're doing it wrong.

Very hot flames on BBQ are actually considered plasma.

> ## The nourishment from barbecue is palatable.

Millard Fillmore

BBQ Dress Code

No Shirt.
No Shoes.
No Problem.

Hot Smoking

Meat cooked above a wood fire, over *indirect heat*, at temperatures between 120 and 180°F (50 and 80°C).

Smoke Cooking

(proper barbecue)

Cooking meat over *indirect heat* at higher temperatures, often in the range of 250°F (121°C).

66

I'm the kind of guy who likes to sit in a greasy spoon and wonder, 'Gee, should I have the T-bone steak or the jumbo rack of BBQ ribs with the side order of gravy fries?' I want high cholesterol. I wanna eat bacon and butter and buckets of cheese, okay?

99

Denis Leary

66

We black. We all family. Especially when it comes to barbecue.

99

Poetic Justice, 1993

The word "heat" comes from the Greek *therma*.

Therma is the name of a Greek town famous for its radioactive hot springs.

"

I love this burger so
much I want to sew
my ass shut.

"

Barney, *How I Met Your Mother,*
'The Best Burger in New York'

As legend tells it, and Google, it was in 1830, that Skilton Dennis, from Otter Town, North Carolina, began the U.S.'s first commercial barbecue establishment.

He started selling pit-cooked hog meat and cornbread from the back of his wagon. Otter Town is now known as Ayden, one of the nation's BBQ hotspots.

Source: Ayden BBQ.org

66

A fine lot of
Barbecue Sauce.
For fresh meats of
all kinds it cannot
be excelled.

99

The first mention of "barbecue sauce." *Bolivar Bulletin*,
Hardeman County, Tennessee, 1871
Source: Amazing Ribs.com

Give thanks to British man John Walker, for it was he who, in 1826, invented the first friction match. For his creation, Walker dipped a thin stick of wood in potassium chlorate paste and sulfur and, when dry, dragged it across sandpaper.

Today, 500 billion matches are used each year, about the same number most amateur chefs use when lighting their BBQs.

Source: BBC

President
George Washington loved
barbecue. On May 27,
1769, he wrote in his diary,
"Went in to Alexandria [VA]
to a barbicue* and stayed
all night."

Must have been a good one.

Source: Amazing Ribs.com

Washington was a notoriously awful speller.

CHAPTER
THREE

Commander -in-Beef

From presidents to princes, paupers to plebs, and everyone in between, everyone on earth is united by the same language: The language of barbecue.

It is as universal as the heavens above and the flames below. But, as that bumper sticker you once saw read: Good guys go to heaven— bad boys barbecue in hell!

In September 18, 1793, after the groundbreaking ceremony for the placing of the cornerstone of the United States Capitol—a huge moment in U.S. history—George Washington celebrated by hosting a barbecue.

The highlight of the day was not the beginning of U.S. democracy, but a 500lb ox roasting over the coals.

Source: History.com

Barbecue Belt

The four most popular types of barbecue cooking in the U.S. are represented by their places of origin. They are known as America's Barbecue Belt.*

1. North Carolina style (vinegar-and-mustard-based sauce)

2. Texas style (sweet and spicy tomato-based sauce)

3. Kansas City style (tangy and thick ketchup-based sauce)

4. Memphis style (sweet and thin tomato-based sauce)

Undone after eating, obviously.

Baby back ribs are called "baby" because they are shorter and quicker to cook than spare ribs.

Commander-in-Beef

Lyndon B. Johnson, the 36th president of the United States, was the first president to host an official barbecue at the White House.

He wanted Texas-style barbecued ribs. Ever since, every other president has hosted official cookouts (for a good cause) on the South Lawn.

Source: Buzzfeed

In 1920, Henry Ford, he of the automobile, created a BBQ briquette from the wood scraps and sawdust from his car factory.

His briquette, combined with his popularity, helped popularize briquettes at BBQs.

Source: Henry Ford.org

Fifty billion burgers were eaten in the U.S. in 2020. This equates to three burgers a week for every single person in the country.

Source: Huffington Post

60 percent of Americans say they barbecue all year-round.

Source: Heart, Patio, and Barbecue Association (HPBA)

Know Thy Rib

There are four types of rib that amateur BBQers need to know:

Spare
(The most common type of rib. Cut from the underbelly of the pig.)

St. Louis style
(No breastbone.)

Country style
(Highest meat-to-bone ratio.)

Baby back
(Least amount of fat.)

Source: Buzzfeed

Warm Your Hands

While this technique may have been debunked by pitmasters for not being accurate enough for their specific tastes, you can roughly measure the heat of your barbecue with your hand.

Hold your hand above your BBQ. The amount of time you can keep it there tells you the temperature.

2-4 seconds: 450-550°F (232-287°C)
5-7 seconds: 350-450°F (176-232°C)
8-10 seconds: 250-350°F (121-176°C)

Source: Weber

"

Southern barbecue is the
closest thing we have
in the U.S. to Europe's
wines or cheeses; drive
a hundred miles and the
barbecue changes.

"

John Shelton Reed

The world's most popular restaurant, McDonald's was, originally, a barbecue drive-in called . . . "McDonald's Bar-B-Que." It opened on May 15, 1940 in San Bernardino.*

Source: Business Insider

Interestingly, McDonald's only roll out their beloved McRib sandwich when pork prices are low.

The seventh president of the United States, Andrew Jackson was nicknamed "Old Hickory," as he was considered as tough as hickory wood, a common smoky wood found at barbecues.

As president, Jackson would hand out hickory toothpicks at his hickory-smoked barbecues.

Source: Thrillist

"

When it's all going swimmingly, the sun's out and I've got a fire going and a nice snake on the barbecue.

"

Bear Grylls

Rest Your Meat

In order to not lose any of the flavorsome juices still present in your meat after cooking, *rest your meat.*

The golden rule of thumb is five minutes per inch of meat thickness, or 10 minutes per pound.

Source: Australian Beef

In June 2012, boxer Mike Tyson endorsed his former rival Evander Holyfield's brand of BBQ sauce on Twitter, by referencing the time he bit off of his ear during the now-iconic Bite Fight.

"@Holyfield's ear would've been much better with his new BBQ sauce," he tweeted.

Source: Twitter

The first collected evidence of human beings cooking meat by flame was found in Wonderwerk Cave, South Africa—approximately one million years ago—the era when human's ancestors, *Homo erectus*, roamed the land.

Source: *New Scientist*

Like a good marriage, barbecue is all about the long, lingering smoke, not the intense flames of passion.

Barbecue is best cooked slowly at temperatures ranging from about 175 to 300°F (80 to 150°C) with more smoke than fire.

If you're gonna go, *go low and slow*.

"

Good barbecue is
more complicated
than you think.

"

Manish Dayal

"

Barbecue is to North
Carolina as the hot
dog is to New York.

"

Fiona Barton

Barbecues aren't just about red and white meat. With a pizza stone, you can cook a pizza on the barbie, too. The circular stones sit on top of the grill and heat up the pizza dough evenly.

In 2019, $1.36 billion worth of grills and barbecues were sold in the United States, an increase from $1.21 billion in 2009.

Source: Statista

68 percent of Americans don't need a special occasion to fire up their barbecues. As long as the sun's out, the buns out!

Source: Statista

66

Summer afternoon;
to me those have always
been the two most
beautiful words in the
English language.

99

Henry James

BBQ Hack

Serve your selection of BBQ condiments—mustard, mayo, ketchup, BBQ sauce, hot sauce, relish, etc.—in a muffin pan. It is a great way to serve all the condiments to your guests at once, while also being portable.

According to a 2019 survey, the most popular foods on the grill are burgers with 85 percent, followed by steak at 80 percent, hot dogs at 79 percent, and chicken at 73 percent.

Source: Hearth, Patio, and Barbecue Association (HPBA)

23 percent
of Americans celebrate Super Bowl
Sunday with a BBQ.

14 percent
of Americans throw a BBQ on
Thanksgiving.

10 percent
of Americans throw a BBQ on
Christmas Day.

9 percent
host a BBQ on New Year's Day.

Source: Statista

In a 2020 survey on why
people eat BBQ,
68 percent of Americans said
it was because of the flavor,
45 percent said lifestyle,
33 percent said convenience,
32 percent said
entertainment, and 19 percent
said because it's a hobby.

Source: GlobeNewswire

In the U.S., 49 percent of all birthday parties are barbecues.

Source: Statista

Worldwide, Weber and Coleman are the two biggest BBQ brands, occupying 40.83 percent and 8.36 percent market share separately.

Source: BBQ Grills Market Report

> **"**
>
> One must maintain
> a little bit of summer,
> even in the middle
> of winter.
>
> **"**

Henry David Thoreau

The United States leads the global market share of BBQ sales.

45 percent of all BBQ sales are in America.

Europe came second, with a 27 percent share of the market.

Source: GlobeNewswire

In 2019, the global barbecue grill market was valued at approximately $5.1 billion.

The value is expected to increase to $8.1 billion by 2023.

Source: Statista

66

Playing with fire is bad for those who burn themselves. For the rest of us, it is a very great pleasure.

99

Jerry Smith

95 percent of
Americans love
everything about
barbecues.

Source: GlobeNewswire

75 percent of U.S. grill owners love to barbecue in the winter.

Source: GlobeNewswire

Samuel Johnson's esteemed 1756 dictionary wasn't particularly definitive about the subject:

66

Barbecue: A hog dressed whole.

99

In 2012, to commemorate a foreign state visit, President Barack Obama gave then-British Prime Minister David Cameron a premium $1,895 Engelbrecht 1000 Braten grill

The grill had a plaque of the U.K. and U.S. flags custom-engraved on the utility shelf.

It was Henry Perry, in 1907, who first brought barbecue to the now-iconic Barbecue Capital of the World—Kansas City. Perry opened a small alley stand and sold smoked meat to workers in the city's Garment District.

Source: *The Martin City Telegraph*

66

To poke a wood fire is more solid enjoyment than almost anything else in the world.

99

Charles Dudley Warner

In November 2020, following the U.S. Election, a Donald Trump supporter in Clark County, Nevada, became an internet sensation when he interrupted a press conference to shout baseless claims that Trump had won the election.

His t-shirt simply read:

BEER. BBQ. FREEDOM.

Top Ten States for BBQ*

1. Montana
2. Kansas
3. Missouri
4. Wyoming
5. Oklahoma
6. Tennessee
7. South Carolina
8. Arkansas
9. Louisiana
10. Alabama

Source: Zippia

Based on amount of restaurants per capita.

> 66
>
> I updated my grilling app, iGrill, today and it now has Facebook integration that lets you see what other people are grilling right now around the world. Awesome.
>
> 99

Mark Zuckerberg

"

I am a great eater of beef, and I believe that does harm to my wit.

"

William Shakespeare

Before the Civil War, Southerners ate, on average, five pounds of pork for every one pound of beef.

Source: *Smithsonian Magazine*

BBQ Hack

Add a small knob of cold butter at the center of your homemade burgers. As the burger cooks, the butter will melt, making the burger twice as juicy and succulent!

66

Any of us would kill
a cow, rather than
not have beef.

99

Samuel Johnson

CHAPTER
FOUR

Sun's Out, Buns Out

There is no great feeling than standing around a BBQ on a sunny afternoon, surrounded by your nearest and dearest.

It is the perfect unison of good food, good people, and good times and, if you're lucky, good weather.

The Humble Bun

An average hamburger bun has a diameter of four inches. This is the same width as most people's hands measured across their bottom knuckles (without the thumb). Look at your hand and see!

66

Give them great
meals of beef and
iron and steel, they
will eat like wolves
and fight like devils.

99

William Shakespeare

Know Thy Meat

Cheaper cuts of beef—shin, flank, chuck, silverside—are best suited to indirect, low and slow barbecue smoking.

Prime cuts —sirloin, T-bone, entrecôte, porterhouse— benefit from faster, more direct grilling.

Heinz sells more than 650 million bottles—and 11 billion sauce sachets—of its ketchup, to more than 140 countries, every year.

Source: Heinz

Homemade Tomato Ketchup*

No BBQ is complete without the world's most popular condiment—ketchup!

Ingredients

$2\frac{1}{4}$lbs (1kg) tomatoes, chopped

9oz (250g) apple, cored and chopped

1 small onion, peeled and chopped

1 clove garlic, peeled

1 small red chili, split

1 cup (200g) sugar

3 tbsps sea salt flakes

7fl oz (200ml) malt vinegar

Tied in a muslin bag: Two whole black peppercorns, one whole allspice, one clove, one star anise

Make It Right

Simmer all the ingredients for two hours.
Discard the spice bag. Pass through a
strainer, then blend until smooth.
Decant into a bottle or jar. Done.

Obviously, Heinz is still the best.

BBQ Hack

Run out of firelighters?

Don't worry . . . we've got your coals covered.

Fill an empty cardboard egg carton with coals, then light the entire carton in the center of your grill. This will get the fire started, without the need for lighter fluid or firelighters.

"

A hot dog at the
game beats roast
beef at the Ritz.

"

Humphrey Bogart

Know Thy Cow

Chuck: Shoulder; tough but flavorful

Shank: Leg; very tough and chewy

Brisket: Breast; tough if not cooked properly

Rib: Rib area; very tender and flavorful

Short plate: Belly; chewy and quite tough

Flank: Abdominal muscles; one of the toughest cuts

Loin: Back, and above the ribs; one of the tenderest cuts

Sirloin: Back, past the loin; pretty tender and flavorful

The round: Back, above the back legs; chewy and tough

Source: Delishably.com

128

Know Thy Steak

Flap: Chewy and fibrous

Filet mignon: Tender and flavorful

Porterhouse: Tender and easy to chew

Skirt/flank: Flavorful but chewy

New York strip: Tough but flavorful

T-Bone: Smooth and savory

Rib-Eye: Tasty and tender, and high in fat

Source: Delishably.com

How to Cook a Steak

Reverse Sear

(indirect heat); best for larger cuts of meat

Slowly cook your steak on indirect heat. Then when it's cooked to your preference in the middle, turn up the heat and sear the exterior.

Hot and Fast

(direct heat); best for single steaks and smaller cuts of meat

Sear the steak over direct heat for a minute or two on each side, then place steak on indirect heat until its done just the way you like it.

66

The smell of roasting meat together with that of burning fruit wood and dried herbs, as voluptuous as incense in a church, is enough to turn anyone into a budding gastronome.

99

Claudia Roden

"

Hamburgers, hamburgers, hamburgers hot;

onions in the middle, pickle on top.

Makes your lips go flippity flop.

"

The chant of one of the U.S. first hamburger vendors, circa 1885. Source: Petit Chef.com

66

The man who invented the hamburger was smart; the man who invented the cheeseburger was a genius.

99

Matthew McConaughey

Cook It Right

Steak doneness is a matter of personal taste.
How do you like yours?

Blue:
One minute per side

Rare:
One and a half minutes per side

Medium rare:
Two minutes per side

Medium:
Two minutes and 20 seconds per side

Well-done:
Four minutes and 30 seconds per side

Source: BBC

> If God did not intend for us to eat animals, then why did he make them out of meat?

John Cleese

BBQ Hack

Want to create those perfect diamond grill marks on your steak?

Easy. Place your steak on the grill so that it points to 10:00 on an imaginary clock. Don't lift the meat until its seared properly.

Then, rotate your steak (on the same side) so that it points to 2:00 on an imaginary clock. Repeat the process on the other side.

"

Not eating meat is a decision, eating meat is an instinct.

"

Denis Leary

Season your meat
no less than an hour
before grilling in
order to lock in the
maximum amount
of flavor.

66

My favorite animal is steak.

99

Fran Lebowitz

CHAPTER
FIVE

Red, White, and Barbecue

The barbecue is the American Dream in food form. Anyone, from sea to shining sea, can do it.

It's the best taste in the world. And— here's the kicker—it feels like a guilty pleasure, when it is one of cleanest and healthiest ways to cook food. Barbecue, we salute you!

"

The only time to eat diet food is while you're waiting for the steak to cook.

"

Julia Child

One fifth of Americans light up their BBQs once a week.

Source: Statista

11 percent of grill owners in the U.S. prepare breakfast on their BBQs.

Source: Forbes

In 2020, the National Hot Dog and Sausage Council revealed that hot dog etiquette decreed, for those 18 years of age and older, acceptable wiener toppings include ONLY mustard, relish, onions, cheese, and chili. Ketchup is a sin.

❝

Let me put it this way, putting ketchup on a hot dog is not acceptable past the age of eight.

❞

Barack Obama

Homemade BBQ Sauce Recipe

Ingredients

1 tbsp olive oil

1 onion, finely chopped

14.5oz (400g) can chopped tomatoes

3 garlic cloves, finely chopped

1/3 cup (85g) brown sugar

3 tbsps malt vinegar

2 tbsps Worcestershire sauce

1 tbsp tomato purée

Salt and pepper, to season

Make It Right

Heat oil in a saucepan and cook the onion over a gentle heat until softened.

Add the remaining ingredients, season, and mix. Bring to a boil, then reduce heat and simmer until thickened.

For a smooth sauce, simply whizz the mixture in a food processor for a few seconds.

Source: BBC

Homemade Mustard Recipe

Mustard is a most welcome friend at a BBQ, second only to ketchup.

Ingredients

1 cup yellow mustard seeds
5fl oz (150ml) cider vinegar
5fl oz (150ml) white wine
Salt
4–5 sprigs of fresh tarragon

Make It Right

Add the mustard seeds, vinegar, white wine, and two teaspoons of salt in a glass bowl and cover with wrap.

Set somewhere cool for three days. On the third day, whizz all the ingredients in a food processor (picking the tarragon leaves first) and blitz until smooth.

Keep in a sealed jar.

Source: Jamie Oliver

"

Then there is the beefsteak. They have it in Europe, but they don't know how to cook it.

"

Mark Twain

27 percent of U.K. barbecuers admitted to never trying to expand their barbecue repertoire outside of the staples—steak, burger, chicken.

Source: *The Sun*

"

I call this turf and turf.
It's a 16-ounce T-Bone and a
24-ounce Porterhouse. Also a
whiskey and a cigar.
I am going to consume all of this
at the same time because I am
a free American.

"

Ron Swanson, *Parks and Recreation,* **'Sweetums'**

Know Thy Mustard

71 percent of Americans eat their hot dogs with traditional yellow mustard, but there are alternatives that add that little bit extra . . .

Yellow mustard:
Traditional hot dog mustard; mild flavor

Dijon mustard:
Sharp and spicy

Spicy brown mustard:
Hot and earthy; ideal for rich, salty meats like pastrami and sausages

Honey mustard:
One to one ratio; heat and sweet

Wholegrain mustard:
Deep and rich

Source: Hot Dog.org

The mesquite tree is native to the southwestern U.S. states and Mexico and it is the key component to Texas-style BBQ.

The wood gives meats a light and sweet flavor.

Know Thy Wood Smoke

For an additional hit of smoky flavor, throw a selection of these chips on your next BBQ. You'll never barbecue without them again . . .

Hickory

Red oak

Mesquite

Apple wood

Cherry wood

Pecan tree

"

When the going gets tough, the tough eat ribs.

"

Nora Roberts

BBQ Hack

Thirty minutes after you've finished using your grill, when the BBQ is a lot cooler but still has some heat, lay down a few sheets of water-soaked newspaper and close the lid. Leave it shut for 30 minutes. This will give your BBQ a steam clean.

Source: Garden Buildings Direct

"

Sex is good, but not as good as fresh, sweet corn.

"

Garrison Keillor

"

Eat beef.
The West wasn't won
on salad.

"

North Dakota Beef Council advertisement, 1990

Lockhart, Texas, became so famous for BBQ that the state senate officially named it the "BBQ Capital of Texas" in 2003.

Pat Your Meat Dry!

Before your meat meets heat, make sure you remember to pat it dry in order to form the best crust and grilling marks.

BBQ Mythbuster

Only Flip Steaks Once

Nonsense.

Frequent flipping will prevent your steak from curling up on the sides and ensure an even cook.

Clean your just-used grill with an onion attached to a fork. Rub the onion over the hot bars.

The water in the onion will steam clean the bars and remove any leftover bits of food you haven't nibbled at.

You should clean your grill racks and utensils after every cookout.

Source: Garden Buildings Direct

Stick and Rip

Remember: It is the heat of the BBQ, not the oil on the meat, that makes the cooking surface nonstick. Resist the urge to flip your meat until it's seared properly, to ensure your meat doesn't stick and rip from the grill.

66

Life expectancy would grow by leaps and bounds if green vegetables smelled as good as bacon.

99

Doug Larson

The Maillard Reaction

Why does BBQ taste so good?

One answer:
The Maillard Reaction

This chemical reaction between amino acids and reducing sugars in the meat gives grilled food its distinctive toasty, malty, and robust flavor.

Source: Serious Eats.com

It takes about 30 minutes for a barbecue to become a cookable temperature.

Coincidentally, this is the same amount of time, health experts agree, that it should take to drink a bottle of beer, and how long it takes the body to feel the first effects of that beer.

Source: Bradford Health.com

66

Nobody, I mean nobody, puts ketchup on a hot dog.

99

Clint Eastwood (as Dirty Harry)

Beer and BBQ

A cold refreshing beer is the best antidote to help balance out all the salt and fats of the barbecue. But you knew that already. These are the bestselling U.S. beer brands in 2020.

10. Busch

9. Busch Light

8. Natural Light

7. Modelo Especial

6. Corona Extra

5. Michelob Ultra

4. Budweiser

3. Miller Lite

2. Coors Light

1. Bud Light

Source: *USA Today*

80 percent of American consumers agree that potato salad is the perfect side dish to a barbecue, followed by green salad and baked potatoes.

Source: Statista

Five of every six grills involved in home fires are fueled by gas, not charcoal.

Source: National Fire Protection Association (NFPA)

BBQ Playlist #1:
Fire

1. *We Didn't Start the Fire*—Billy Joel
2. *Great Balls of Fire*—Jerry Lee Lewis
3. *Fire and Rain*—James Taylor
4. *Light My Fire*—The Doors
5. *Sex on Fire*—Kings of Leon
6. *Burning down the House*—Talking Heads
7. *Play with Fire*—Rolling Stones
8. *Smoke on the Water*—Deep Purple
9. *Ring of Fire*—Johnny Cash
10. *Keep the Fire Burnin'*—REO Speedwagon

66

Love and sausage are
alike. Can never have
enough of either.

99

Dean Koontz

CHAPTER
SIX

The Whole Hog

The best thing about barbecues is that they last for hours. They are not a wham-bam-thank-you-man type of social event, much like the low and slow method itself.

Indeed, barbecues are not about how long they take, but about how slow time feels while they're happening.

To quote that great American icon Ferris Bueller, "Life moves pretty fast. If you don't slow down and look around you might miss it." Amen.

BBQ Playlist #2: Classic Cuts

1. *Steak for Chicken*—Moldy Peaches

2. *Eat That Chicken*—Charles Mingus

3. *Shake Hands with Beef*—Primus

4. *The Burger Song*—Skee-Lo

5. *Meat Man*—Jerry Lee Lewis

6. *Texas Cookin'*—Guy Clark

7. *Meat City*—John Lennon

8. *Cheeseburger in Paradise*—Jimmy Buffett

9. *Hot Dog*—Led Zeppelin

10. *Hot Dogs and Hamburgers*—John Mellencamp

Mortuusequusphobia
(The fear of ketchup)

Lachanophobia
(The fear of vegetables)

Cenosillicaphobia
(The fear of an empty glass)*

*Nobrewphobia—*the fear of running out of beer.*
Sadly not a real phobia.

Americans eat 20 billion hot dogs every year. That's about 70 hot dogs per U.S. citizen.

Do you down a dog that often?

Source: *USA Today*

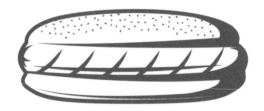

Cheers, Coal!

Charcoal was one of man's very first inventions, dating back more than 200,000 years. Today, lump wood charcoal—hardwoods such as oak and cherry are typically used—is made by burning wood at 1000°F without the presence of oxygen. This methodical charring removes water and chemical compounds from the wood, leaving a carbon-rich product.

Source: Serious Eats.com

The American form of the charcoal briquette, as it is known today, was first invented and patented by Ellsworth B. A. Zwoyer of Pennsylvania in 1897.

Source: South Florida Reporter

All Hail, Joey Chestnut!

In July 2020, at Nathan's world-famous Hot Dog Eating Contest in New York, Californian Joey Chestnut broke his own world record for the most hot dogs eaten in less than ten minutes—75!

Why not try and break that record at your next BBQ?

Source: *The New York Times*

65 percent of Americans would support bacon as their national food.

Source: Smithfield.com

The Wurst

There are an estimated 1,500 varieties of German sausage. All of them are the wurst— bratwurst, blutwurst, knackwurst, lebetrwurst, teewurst, gelbwurst, weisswurst, to name a few. The humble frankfurter, from Frankfurt, is the king of American hot dogs.

The Hangover

High-protein foods such as burgers, steak, and bacon can help your body fight off a hangover.

So, in theory, you should never get a hangover at a BBQ. Right?

Source: Healthline.com

"

Heaven sends us
good meat but the
Devil sends cooks.

"

David Garrick

Carnivore

Eats only meat.

Carnival

A time of intense merrymaking before the removal of all meat from one's diet (i.e. Lent).

Hot Guts

The technical term for sausages (in Texas). Also: Hot Links.

Mustard Tears

That first annoying dribble of clear liquid that comes out of a mustard bottle if you forget to shake it first.

Pig Pickin'

A BBQ roast where a whole hog is served on a spit and guests can feel free to just pick whatever part of the pig they want. Forks are forbidden.

POGS:
Steak Seasoning

Seasoning is a matter of taste, but for those who like to KISS (keep it simple, stupid), just remember POGS . . .

1 tbsp black pepper (P)

1 tbsp onion powder (O)

2 tbsps garlic powder (G)

2 tbsps sea salt flakes (S)

Done.

If you want a way to grill chicken that will impress your friends, try Beer Can Chicken.

Crack open a cold can of beer, stick it inside a whole chicken, and place it vertically on searing white-hot coals. Close the lid.

The smoke and heat will cook the chicken, and the juices of the beer will boil and baste the chicken, ensuring it stays juicy and succulent.

Pitmaster

A barbecue expert;
an artist;
a master craftsperson;
a God among mortals.

Probably has a beard.